Personalities of The Zodiac
A Cartoon Chronicle on How Your Birthday Shapes Your Character

Written and Illustrated by William Schreib

Dedicated to the years of my parents' kindness

Special thanks to Janice Michael and Marwayne Leipzig
for their astrological insights, to Loretta Jean, Judi Fix
and Pearl Foster for their editing and continuity contributions,
and to Steve Oliver for his publishing consultation.

All rights reserved. No part of this book may be reproduced or transmitted in
any form or by any means, electronic or mechanical, including photocopying,
recording or by any information storage and retrieval system without written
permission from the author, except for the inclusion of brief quotations in a review.
ISBN 0-9614627-0-1
Library of Congress Catalog Card Number: 98-90335
FIRST PRINTING

Copyright 1998 by William A. Schreib
Starry-Eyed Productions
P.O. Box D
Culdesac, Idaho 83524 USA

Forward and Onward

We really got something here! In the vastness of this Universe, there are countless galaxies. Like our own Milky Way, most of these galaxies are likely to contain over a hundred million stars -- and at least a million solar systems. And at this point, so far as we know, none of them have a planet as unique as our blessed Earth.

Earth is not only ideally placed, it also has some distinctive "life-inducing" mechanisms. Its daily spin gives a perfectly timed offering of light and darkness. The oceans, lakes and pools are stirred by the tug of lunar forces. The planet's axis-tilt transforms the yearly trip around the sun into a cyclic ride of four delightful "seasonal experiences". All of these heavenly factors have undeniably influenced the creation of life on this planet.

At some magic moment in primordial time, those wondrous concoctions of conditions inspired and sparked consciousness. Was it (as some suppose) that the Universe's Creator simply followed a master plan creating Earth for Man? Or did Man evolve because the variable array of cycles provided "just the right conditions"? However you believe, we are still part of a truly remarkable evolutionary process!

Astrology is the language that defines the relationships between these conditions on Earth and in the Heavens. As the title implies, this book attempts to show how astrology and the yearly seasonal patterns affect the nature and inherent makeup of its living creatures -- plants, animals and notably, its people. In this cartoon chronicle, it's all there to see-- as the year unfolds!

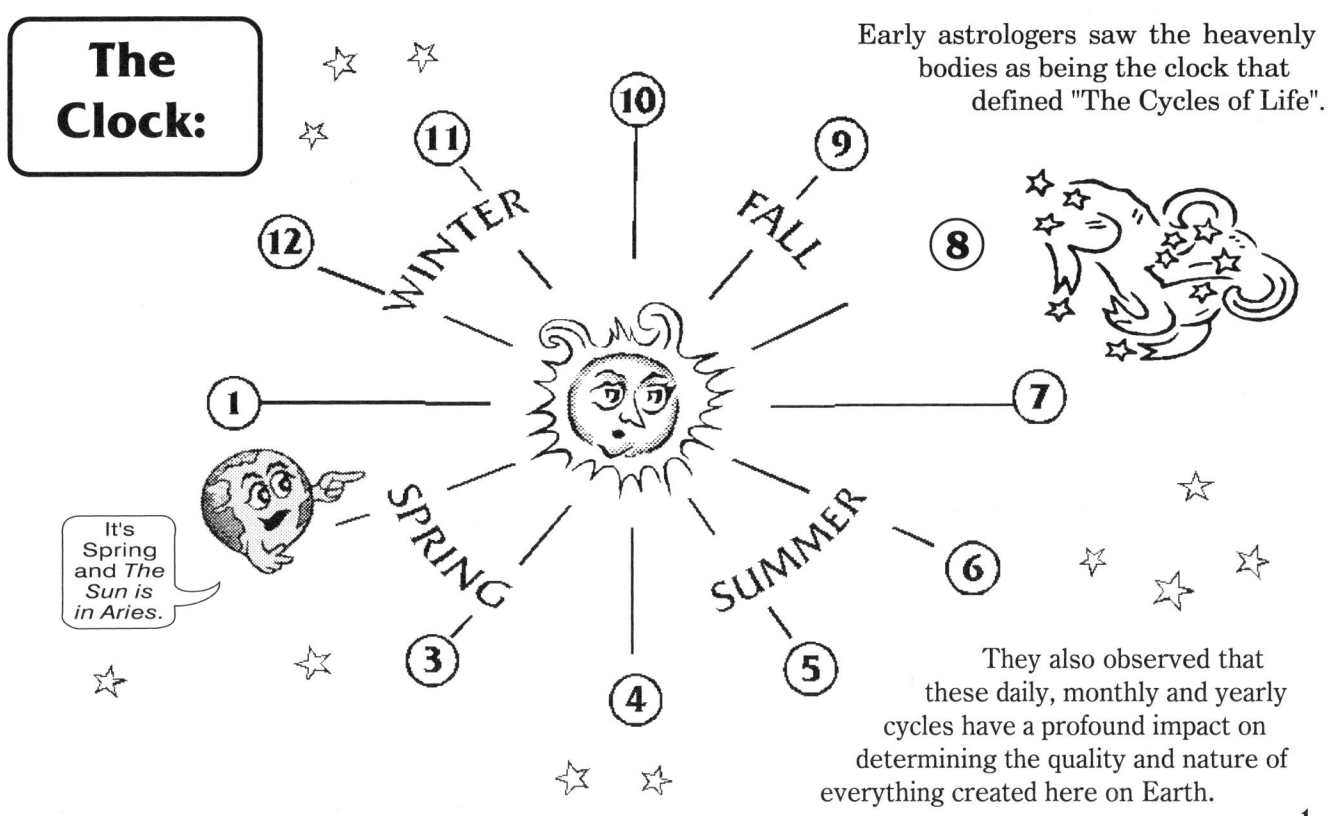

> **The Modes:**
> "Whipping things into shape"

The most consistent and influential cycle occurs when the Earth orbits around the Sun *and the seasons appear in a regular pattern:*

1. *Each Season moves in --*

2. *Lies Dormant...*

3. *...then Changes!*

Like clockwork, this three-step procedure repeats itself as it molds and shapes the four seasons, throughout the years.

These three "shaping forces" are known as the **Astrological Modes:**

Cardinal

They *Stretch...*

At each Solstice and Equinox point, everything is propelled to "move" in a new direction.

▼

Aries
Cancer
Libra
Capricorn

Fixed

SQUEEZE ...

All those "Caught-in-the-Middle" have an urge to consolidate and put things on hold.

▼

Taurus
Leo
Scorpio
Aquarius

Mutable

Twist & Turn!

When the seasons begin to change, it's time to make some alterations.

▼

Gemini
Virgo
Sagittarius
Pisces

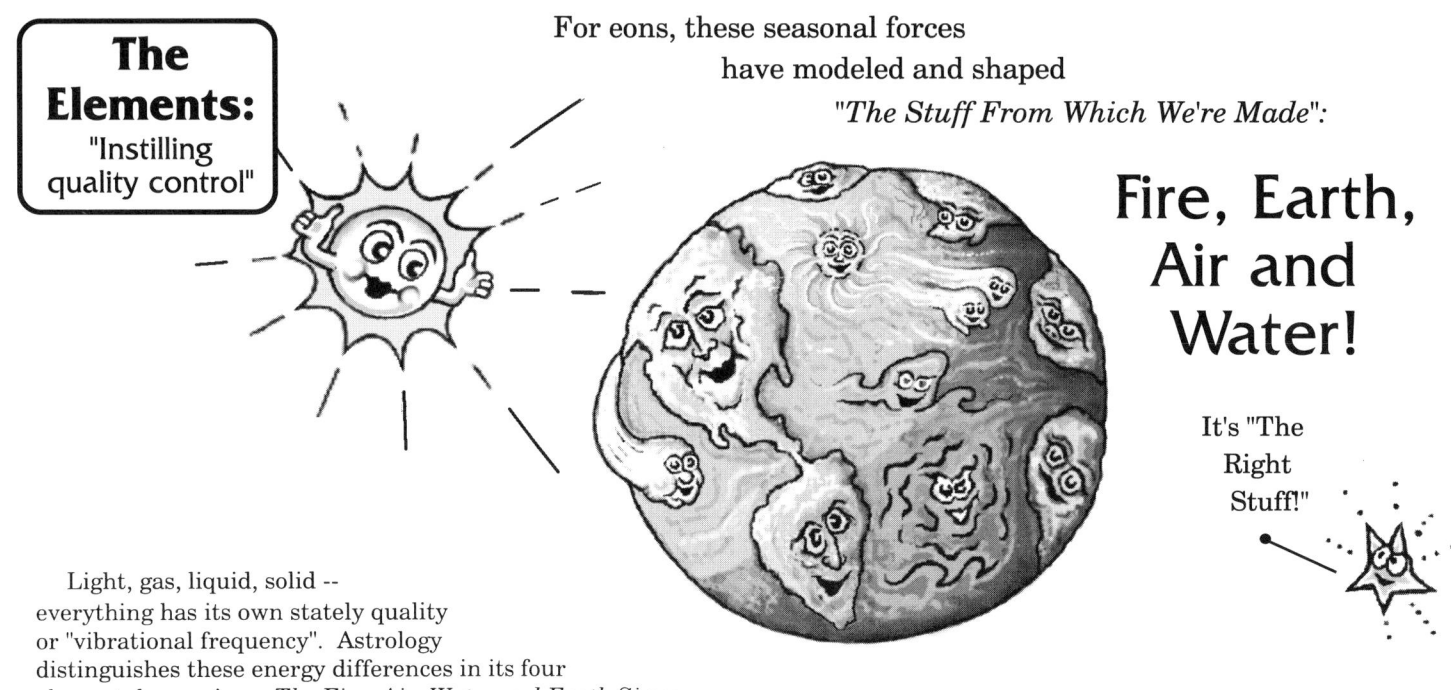

The Elements:
"Instilling quality control"

For eons, these seasonal forces have modeled and shaped *"The Stuff From Which We're Made"*:

Fire, Earth, Air and Water!

It's "The Right Stuff!"

Light, gas, liquid, solid -- everything has its own stately quality or "vibrational frequency". Astrology distinguishes these energy differences in its four elemental groupings: *The Fire, Air, Water and Earth Signs*.

Respectively, these elements also correspond to the spirit, mind, soul and body of living beings, symbolizing their spiritual, mental, psychic and physical states of consciousness.

When stretched, squeezed and twisted by the seasonal forces, each element is given three ways to show "the mettle of its making". And of course, with four elements, this results in twelve configurations of frequency and shape. Symbolically, these energy patterns portray a dozen archetypal expressions as well as the twelve-step program found in a year's cycle of creation. On the celestial clock, they appear as *The Zodiac Signs*.

Fire: Aries, Leo, Sagittarius

In the heat of the moment, the **Fire Signs** find three highly spirited modes of expression. The actions are sharp, quick and even noticeable in the flick of an eye.

Autumn turns into a wintry chill when the **Mutable-Fire** of SAGITTARIUS scatters the "remaining heat" across the land.

By mid-Summer, the heat is contained, as LEO's furnace of **Fixed-Fire** extrudes the warmth from the glowing embers.

When Spring rushes in, flames ignite and spread as the **Cardinal-Fire** of ARIES burns away the clutter.

Earth: Taurus, Virgo, Capricorn

The **Earth Signs** follow and counter each fiery flare with their substantial and stabilizing works— remodeling the ash and clay into the physical shape of each sign's astrological mode.

To prepare for Fall, VIRGO rearranges **Mutable-Earth's** Harvest into serviceable forms.

In mid-Spring, roots sink deep into **Fixed-Earth** so that TAURUS can build bulk and form.

The **Cardinal-Earth** of CAPRICORN moves the essential goodies into useful piles, to sustain life through winter's cold.

Air: Gemini, Libra, Aquarius

The preceding physical sensations expand into streams of thought, when the **Air Signs** follow the currents of prevailing winds.

At the Fall Equinox, the **Cardinal Air** of LIBRA moves the high and low weather fronts into tranquil balance.

At the first seasonal change of the year, GEMINI's **Mutable-Air** stirs up a storm, scattering the dust in the wind.

In the doldrums of winter, the funneling effect of the **Fixed-Air** of AQUARIUS gives a calm centering eye, surrounded by the chaos of a hurricane.

Water:
Cancer, Scorpio, Pisces

All of the previous creations are conjoined into meaningful wholes by the emotional tugs of the three **Water Signs.**

When the nights run long, the life forces still. In the icey **Fixed Water** of SCORPIO they are contained and regenerated.

At the Summer Solstice, the surging tides of CANCER'S **Cardinal Waters** send the emotions running in new directions.

As snows melt, then evaporate and fall as recycling rains, the **Mutable Water** of PISCES prepares all levels of life for the coming changes of Spring.

In the annual turn of events, the changing polarities, daily and monthly cycles, and transiting planets create a countless mix of combinations. However, *"the reason for the season"* remains simple and unaltered-- and it is played out in the disposition and personality of each and every newborn living creation. The seasonal sign in position on the day of birth is *"The Sun Sign"*. It determines our perspective on reality and it gives us a *unique gift of expression,* which we can use-- to help bring another year into life!

These are the TRUE PIONEERS.

William Shatner Leonard Nimoy
They go where no one has gone before!

Aries' long triangular face mocks the appearance of a sheep. Note the double-crowned horned hairline, the protruding forebrow and snout, the wide-set eyes (that sweep back and upwards) and the full upper lip that places the mouth low on the chin. Also, the long arched neck makes the "adam's apple" quite prominent.

Ariens have a knack for "getting things started".

"Finishing the task" is someone else's job.

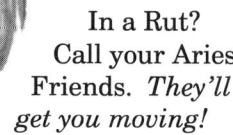

Alex Baldwin,
Christine Lahti,
Eric Clapton,
Elton John,
Janis Ian,
Hugh Hefner,
Bette Davis

In a Rut? Call your Aries Friends. *They'll get you moving!*

IT'S TIME TO BEGIN A NEW ADVENTURE!

Dennis Quaid, Marilou Henner, Warren Beatty, Hugh Hefner, Alex Baldwin, Celine Dion, Joan Crawford, Eddie Murphy, Sarah Jessica Parker, Paul Reiser, Al Gore

More than all other signs, Taureans seem enticed and aroused by the five physical senses.

It gives some of them insatiable appetites:

Catherine The Great, Alice B. Toklas, Dennis Hopper, Liberace and ORSON WELLES

Physical traits include the thick curly hair, the wide fixed brows and bovine eyes, the wide nostrils, the square jaw and the heavy neck and shoulders.

I will drink ALL wine, anytime!

Our Taurean friends help us find ecstasy in the "Simple Stuff" of life.

L. Frank Baum, George Carlin, Audrey Hepburn, Jack Klugman, Jimmy Stewart

"There are so many stimulating things."
Savador Dali, Uma Thurman, Bianca Jagger, George Lucas
"There are so many fixations." — Sigmund Freud

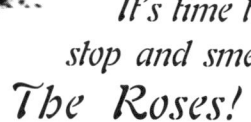

It's time to stop and smell The Roses!

Shirley MacLaine, Michelle Pfieffer, Uma Thurman, Jack Nicholson, Janet Jackson, Glen Campbell, Bea Arthur, Al Pacino, George Clooney, Harry Truman

Gemini's juggling of ideas often results in a prolific output of words.

John Barth, Lilian Hellman, Dr. Ruth Westheimer, Sir Arthur Conan Doyle, Barry Manilow

Their encyclopedic minds seem to know everything.

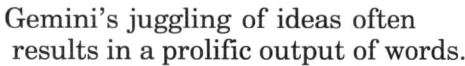

Can we talk?

Joan Rivers

The answer is blowing in the wind.

Bob Dylan

The volume of data can **boggle your mind!**

These quick-witted chatter boxes are sure to add sparks to any conversation.

Gene Wilder, Ally Sheedy, Judy Garland, Judge Reinhold, Chuck Barris, Sharon Gless

Appropriately, Geminis have "twin" facial features and an off-kilter, mutable appearance. There seems to be two lower and upper lips-- and a double layer of eyelids! (The extra folds above the eyelids usually produce "two blinks" instead of one). Note how the long, thin nose and the pointed chin skew off in opposite directions.

Just THINK about the possibilities.

Dr. Ruth, Michael J. Fox, Nicole Kidman, Paul McCartney, John Kennedy, Cyndi Lauper, Sharon Gless, Clint Eastwood, Tim Allen, Marilyn Monroe

At the Solstice, polarities change and Gemini's scattered thoughts are gathered together.

Cancer
June 22 to July 22

At Light's peak, the tides shift and the year begins its long journey into night.

Cardinal Water, like the ebb and flow of the tides, expresses itself in liquid moving surges.

Cancer's emotions are tossed and turned by the Moon's tidal forces.

Cancers emotionally feel that these forces are waning, so they gather in all the resources they can, to secure their comfort zone.

There's No Place Like Home!

With their shells turned to the side, Crabs *lean into the wave*. Regularily, they must step backwards to redirect their forward motion.

About every 2 1/2 days, our moods shift when the Moon enters a new sign.

Cancers beam when the full moon reflects from their rounded "lunar temples".

Barbara Stanwick, Kevin Bacon, James Cagney, Freddie Prinze, Kathy Bates, Natalie Wood

Also watch for the full deep eyes, the high forehead, the wide eyebrow plate and the small recessed jaw.

Underneath Cancer's tranquil surface, the pressures build-- until they erupt like a geyser releasing steam.

Listen for the warbling *lunar cackle*.

Phyllis Diller, Peter Lorre, Ross Perot

The *harmonic waves* of Cancer's soothing voice lifts our moods and keeps us in tune with the rhythms of life.

Linda Ronstadt, Lena Horne, Don Henley, Debbie Harry, Cat Stevens, Carly Simon, Kris Kristofferson, Kim Carnes

At the crest of the wave, the undercurrents pull us in new directions.

David Hasselhoff, Ross Perot, Angelica Huston, Dear Abby, Meryl Streep, Princess Di, Liz McGovern, Chris O'Donnell, George Michael, Bill Cosby

It's time to come out of your shell-- to play and bask in the Sun!

Leo
July 23 to Aug. 22

The long, hot doldrums of Summer seem endless and rich with abundance.

It's enough to instill a sense of confidence.

All of this is for ME!

With a prideful strut, the Lion parades through his kingdom, pronouncing his royal decrees.

The SUN is the source of LEO's glow, as it signifies the dignified arrangement --

-- Everything revolves around the CENTER LIGHT!

So, shine the light on me--

'cuz, I'm one fantastic carrot!

The residual heat of **Fixed Fire** keeps things warm and radiant.

Leos have a magnanimous presence and they attract a lot of attention.

Bill Clinton, Estelle Getty, Robert Mitchum, Linda Ellerbe, Martin Mull, Kathie Lee Gifford

♥

"The Greatest Love of All Is Learning To Love Yourself"

Whitney Houston

♥

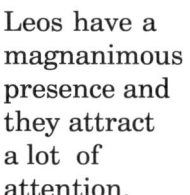

As these lions purr, paw, and preen, all the world becomes a stage on which we all can play.

Steve Martin

Mick Jagger

Lucille Ball

AFTER ALL, WHEN YOU'RE **HOT**, YOU'RE **HOT!**

Watch for the lion's mane, the bushy eyebrows, the feline eyes, the broad and stubby nose, the jowly cheeks and the barrel-chested torso.

Melanie Griffith, Delta Burke, Sally Struthers, Patrick Swayze, Garrison Keillor, Hulk Hogan, Jackie Kennedy, Andy Warhol, Michael Richards, Connie Chung

Keanu Reeves, Tom Skerritt, Peter Falk, Marcia Clark, L.B. Johnson, Lauren Bacall, Shelley Long, Geraldine Ferraro, Peter Sellers, Richard Gere

Angie Dickinson, M. Mantle, John Lithgow, Linda Hamilton, Julie Andrews, Annette Funicello, D. W. Eisenhower, Tim Robbins, Mike Douglas, Cheryl Tiegs

To make room for the valuable other goods, Scorpios know they must eliminate the useless "trash".

Yum, a carrot. I'd better eat it... before it rots.

EEK

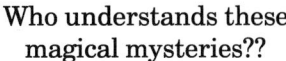
See Scorpio Charlie Bronson take out the garbage!

DEATHWISH VIII
A HEAVY MOVIE!

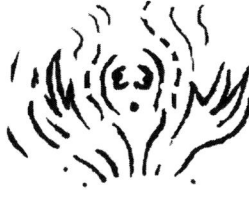
Ya wanna explore biology with me?

Unaffected by the slime and grime, Scorpios make superior surgeons and "bio-explorers".

Jonas Salk, Carl Sagan, Marie Curie

Few heard the screams of the sacrificial carrot as it met its end.

In this moment of silence, we recognize it's miraculous gift:

The carrot has risen from the ashes to be transformed into a new life force.

Who understands these magical mysteries??

BURP

The SCORPIO Knows!

Pablo Picasso, Lauren Holly, Marla Maples Trump, Winona Ryder, Dan Rather, Martin Scorsese, Jane Pauley, Roy Rogers, Prince Charles

Hillary Clinton, Walter Cronkite, Jodie Foster, Danny DeVito, Roseanne, Henry Winkler, Dennis Franz, Leonardo Decaprio, Grace Kelly, Ed Asner

When Sagittarians enact their divine sense of "*seeing beyond all that exists*", they reach beyond the boundaries and discover universal truths.

This expansive perspective can produce a prolific array of philosophic pronouncements.

William F. Buckley, Jr.,
Morton Downey, Jr.,
Phil Donahue,
Don King

It sends some centaurs galloping after distant odysseys and fantasies.

Steven Spielberg,
Walt Disney,
Janine Turner,
Joseph Cambell
Mary Martin

Appropriately, these jovial clowns usually see *"The Lighter Side"* of everything.

Steve Landesberg,
Spike Jones, Flip Wilson,
John Larroquette,
Richard Pryor,
Emmett Kelly

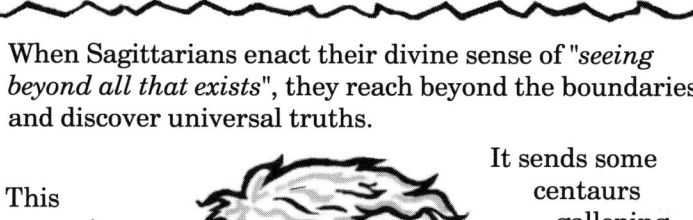

HUH?
GO

Harpo Marx

Some Saggis are so blunt and truthful they repeatedly insert "hoof into mouth".

Gary Hart, Sinead O'Connor, Jane Fonda

The lack of grounding makes many of these creatures noticeably clumsy and awkward.

Wally Cox, Teri Garr,
Woody Allen

43

Woody Allen, Caroline Kennedy, Teri Hatcher, Don Johnson, Dick Van Dyke, Sammy Davis Jr., Bette Midler, Monica Seles, Ed Koch, Frank Sinatra

Faye Dunnaway, Marlene Dietrich, Frank Zappa, John Denver, Mary Tyler Moore, Jean Stapleton, Robert Duvall, George Burns, Anthony Hopkins, John Voit

Clark Gable, Alan Alda, Nick Nolte, Paul Newman, Carol Channing, Cybill Shepherd, Oprah Winfrey, Geena Davis, Burt Reynolds, Tom Selleck

Pisces' impressionable personality bends and weaves with the changing currents.

Some lost souls lose all sense of self as they escape into their delusional worlds.

Others find humor in the bewildering chaos!

Billy Crystal, Erma Bombeck, Kelsey Grammer, Jerry Lewis, Lou Costello

In the shimmering reflections, many discover the joyful blessings that make life "*A Wonder-Filled Experience*".

Sally Jesse Raphael, Dr. Seuss, Mr. Rogers, Ron Howard

Jackie Gleason, Liza Minnelli

Some fish seem to be constantly swimming against the currents.

Tom Arnold, Bruce Willis, Peter Fonda, Drew Barrymore, Jon Bon Jovi, Kato Kaelin, Sharon Stone

It's amazing-- everything works!

It's a miracle-- anything works!

With all of these emotional interactions, Pisceans often feel "*they're in someone else's shoes*". Compassionately, they often sacrifice their personal needs to help others.

George Harrison, Liz Taylor, Ralph Nader, Joanne Woodward, Mikhail Gorbachev, Bernadette Peters

Drew Barrymore, George Harrison, Ted Kennedy, Sally Jessy Raphael, Willard Scott, Bernadette Peters, Bruce Willis, Hal Lynden, Erma Bombeck, Joanne Woodward

and enjoy the years!

For information on other "Starry-Eyed" Productions
write us at P.O. Box D, Culdesac, ID 83524
E-Mail: starry_eyed12   @   hotmail.com